Isle of Sin
Simon Maddrell

for
Alan Shea

—

in memory of
those we lost

polari

Contents

Ware ye navar in love with a boy?   5

i.m. Dursley McLinden (1965–1995)
Bells & Bells   8
i could have been you   9
Remembrance of the Daleks & Other Supernatural Creatures   10
Life was a Trapdoor   11
Poem in August at 5pm   12
a politician walks into a mirrored room   14

Manx Queer History (1986–1992)
MOAS (Manx Opposed to Alan Shea) Manifesto, 1991   15
Standing in his yard looking like Liberace in a velvet jacket   16
Bona Vacantia   17
Pride & Protest   18
Pink & Blue   19
Knock & Pull   20
Spy & Trap   21
Any Excuse   22
Death & Debts   23

Queer & Manx in 2022
Isle of Man Government   24
Isle of Man Constabulary   25
Joe Locke, Manx Actor   26
Young, Queer & Manx   27

Manx LGBT+ Legislative Timeline 1992–2022   28
Notes & Queeries   29
Acknowledgments & Thanks   32

Ware ye navar in love with a boy?

What way?
Well that's the thing I cannot say.
Like a brother or that? No! no! no! no!
T.E. Brown (1830–1897)

I was mad for those two boys,
who became gods, hefting hard
to look so fine, wiry scattered hair,
fragrant thoughts fluttered my mind.

I longed to worship with them
alone, to feel raw & pure lust, and
worship them I did, on my knees,
and my hands you know where

I placed them, rowing in a boat,
the boys stripped — sculpted arms,
necks & backs like barked beech.
I considered their bathing bodies

islands within islands, a desire
for sea in a sea, which I'd once
sunk into the innermost depths,
moving me deeper, below deck

foreheads drip on their open lips,
tongued every time I look. Now
every sinew strains, my eyes trail
the lines of their bulging temples.

O to be in their *lek* — wrestling
naked beauty, where shame lies
and truths grapple — with love
that changes nothing, but love.

lek : an aggregation of males gathered to engage in courtship rituals.

i.m. Dursley McLinden

Manx actor, dancer and singer (1965–1995)

Dursley, who died of AIDS-related illness, was an inspiration for
the character Ritchie Tozer in the Channel 4 drama, *It's A Sin*.

Bells & Bells

You knew what you wanted from a young age adventure was fear to your mother who sewed bells to the toes of your shoes. Drawing due attention, your charm ringing for its own sake. One can get lost in plain ear-sight. Centre stage can be an island entire of itself. And bells finally toll for actors too.

Not all bells were quelled after yours too many other graves left unmarked or planted with trees hiding their truth instead of friends surrounding them when the soil was fresh & ready

i.m. Dursley McLinden (1965–1995)

i could have been you

> born just six months later
> in the same place,
> on the same island.
> even though i can't act or sing or dance
>   — but apart from that, we shared
>
> a common fear of cybermen
> and we couldn't hide
> behind the same sofa
> even though we had the same difference
>   in our way. before *it's a sin* was sung
>
> we tried to escape from shame —
> i hid in a similar island home,
> river-locked in the forest of dean.
> even though i was fifteen years behind
>   your pink-palaced fun and *follies*,
>
> we were *the man most likely to*
> realise our ambitions with *damn*
> *yankees* and a charity to help others.
> even though we juggled so much — we cut
>   friends in half, and we were cut up
>
> too after contracting HIV.
> you a *diamond* in the fatal eighties,
> even though twenty-five years later for me,
>   we played around those safe spaces
>   across from our sexsick island.
>
> even though in the *remembrance of the daleks*
>   you faced them down, *phantomed*
>   the opera* with ten weeks to live.
>   i could never have been you
>   because I used to wish I was dead.

i.m. Dursley McLinden (1965–1995)

Remembrance of the Daleks & Other Supernatural Creatures

At Sgt Mike Smith's funeral
Ace asks The Doctor if they've

done good, to which question,
he says, *time will tell*

how Dursley's acting & AIDS
activism is seen & not seen

how Sylvester remembers his
presence after thirty-four years

seen & not seen, all those deaths,
all those graves, all those stories

retold from The Pink Palace, sin-
painted facts & fictions swirling,

as every Doctor knows — time
does not wait for permission.

i.m. Dursley McLinden (1965–1995)

Life was a Trapdoor

Actors know one's entrance is everything —
the Dark Side being stage left, whilst a Hero's
Journey begins from the opposite side facing us.

But your life was a more complex theatrical
device — six trapdoors that fitted your fate —
The Sunroof portal letting all the light in.

The Star not just on stage, but off-screen too.
The Cauldron of the 80s & 90s some called
AIDS, others hate. The Vampire had a flap.

The Grave may have plunged like your Liquid
Dimmer light, but The Corsican still performs
at the Gaiety Theatre and Opera House, Douglas

allowing your angelic ghost to glide and ascend
across the whole stage — bypassing those
Middle Age exits to Heaven and Hell facing us.

i.m. Dursley McLinden (1965–1995)

Poem in August at 5pm

after Dylan Thomas & Federico García Lorca

He lay still dying, purple
stains encircled by sisters
& mothers — given &
found — a darling lamb

daring to reach sheepdom but
his wool is matted with sweat &
sweaty frolics have seen their last
May — in his thirtieth year to heaven

forgotten mournings beckon him
for another dawn, his natural-born
youthful guise turns to death's mask
like a bull & the bullfighter's cape —

a las cinco de la tarde
a boy brought the white sheet
at five in the afternoon
a bull bellowed through his forehead.

i.m. Dursley McLinden (1965-1995)

A dance floor of funerals at another
place they call The Actors' Church
where Punch & Judy fought below
its portico, thanks to a little magic

the priest is only allowed to say
a little prayer — one hundred follow
the black hearse with black horses
and Judi Dench's black leather

waving him back to Man —
floating on two-hundred pints
of lemonade too late to splash
a furred tongue & scarred throat.

O may his heart's truth still be sung

back home where the fearful
on high hills stumble, and tumble
a spiked barrel down Slieau Whallian
— unknown numbers within.

i.m. Dursley McLinden (1965–1995)

a politician walks into a mirrored room

tells himself with a straight face
that revealing the numbers living with HIV
would shed a bad light

        like mist after dusk over our mountain
           every water drop being an RNA copy
              of each clouded figure

the MHK is fixed upon the medical list —
few gays amongst the fishers & farmers
but all brothers & sisters in blood

        needles shadow an infinity of backs
          this mirror showing our island
            with a condition like his

MHK : Member of the House of Keys, the elected house
of the Manx Tynwald Parliament.

MOAS (Manx Opposed to Alan Shea) Manifesto, 1991

M O A S

We, the MANX O~~WE~~ ALAN SHEA, a group of Local people of the Isle Of Man; do hereby demand that the Manx Government, who were elected by the Manx people, immediately recognise that the Manx people ~~do not~~ wish for Homosexuality to be made legal on our beautiful island.

WE THEREFORE DEMAND THE FOLLOWING -

1 A National survey of the people of the Isle Of Man regarding the Homosexual ~~issue~~ is to be carried out on the Island by an independent body (such as Gallup) to prove once and for all that Manx people ~~do not~~ want the Law changed.

2 MHK's who choose to ignore the results of such a survey immediately resign - if they cannot represent the views of the people who put them into office, then they should not be there.

3 Manx Radio and all other news media, including Border Television, ~~refuse~~ to give Alan Shea ~~any~~ more airtime or space in any column to promote his ~~un~~natural acts.

4 The Manx Government is to ~~take im~~mediate steps to ~~re~~move Alan Shea ~~from the Island and~~ to ensure that he is never allowed to ~~re~~turn ~~again~~.

We also demand that these issues are carried out by the present Manx Government, before the November election.

M O A S
Representing the voice of the Manx.

15

Standing in his yard looking like Liberace in a velvet jacket

Mel Cheetham clings to his pineapples
and palms their stone column
as if his whole masculinity
depended upon them and his desire

to birch homosexuals himself
— *unnatural and utterly disgusting* —
consider this obsession imbalanced
— *just as the spirit level cannot lie* —

Spending too much time prookal magh
those rough fellows sheese y raad
that hardened gardener seose y chronk
backing him up with old Manx tongue.

His detached house is covered in cracks
as if something underneath has slipped.

prookal magh : searching out.
sheese y raad : down the road.
seose y chronk : up the hill.

Bona Vacantia

i.m. Frank Duggan and Dorothy Duggan (née Duggan)

Frank and his sister, unlike any self-respecting
Dorothy, were praying daily for buggery
never to be legal — at least between men.
The intoned teachings of their chaste god mean
their earthly goods have no family to speak of

young boys who can be so easily corrupted.
One go, and you're hooked! — which perhaps is
why Frank grasps a hard-backed bible in one hand
a fisting manual in his other, leaving faeces-
eating tips on his lips — *the island is standing up*

to be counted — except the six gay men falling like
her Latter Rain Mission — the Duggans a parody
of themselves, *The Fast Show* sketch with a stink
of incest inside a caravan that was not allowed.

Bona Vacantia [Latin] : The legal situation when someone dies intestate without dependents whereby the assets transfer to the state.

Pride & Protest

~~I would birch homosexuals.~~
Robin Oake's imported persecution
from across, the striped legs of God's
Copper mince through our cottages.

~~Wimps & perverts infect society further.~~
Allan Bell's striped trousers speak up
in the House of Keys outing *ignorance
bigotry & hypocrisy in awesome sight.*

~~Bum blasters, dirty filthy buggery.~~
Alan Shea's striped pyjama Petition
for Redress. Plain-clothed police jabbed
their fingers, white-capped cadets hissed.

~~The law should not be changed.~~
Bishops of Sodor & Man prayed and
voted as blood striped their arms, hoping
suicides will cleanse queer-stained souls.

across : Great Britain

Pink & Blue

blank sheet of paper / waiting for
an informer's pink ink / blue hounds
sniffed twenty-one queers / three-days
of home-flushing / in that '92 sting

> *we're going for a cigarette*
> *when we come back, we want a list,*
> *names, those known homosexuals*
> *or never see your son again*

two blue fingers point / & tap
ringing the ears of their kin /
cells lit every hour / the rope got tight
a pavement spat / one car fumed

blue came back / with two fags dead
in their own hands / a blank sheet left

Knock & Pull

The marked police car pulled
up at the sixteenth home
on a weekend of raids
after four months of peeping
in those toilets of refuge
secret cameras wreaked
their vengeance.

For most, a knock on the door
was the end of the beginning.
But this one was different.
The bang in the attic came
first. Someone had fallen
& just like that
the trigger had been pulled.

Spy & Trap

The Manx police were handsome-
short to enact their toilet entrapments.
Though when I skeeted at the photo line-
up of young police cadets in the 1980s
I remembered — everything within beauty
and truth is comparative — those days
when honey traps were inside jobs like
The Beverley Sister cops in 60s Earl's Court.

Believe it — or not — there was a pretty boy
from Peel — who the police knew for certain
reasons — arrested in all their cottage stings
but never charged — for whatever purpose, kept
to themselves — as if by magic his full bladder
went to Douglas, and his face stayed at home.

skeeted : looked

Any Excuse

You won't find him in there, says Alan Shea
as the policeman flips the freezer flap in the fridge
looking, they say, for Irish escapee Mad Dog Magee
in such an unlikely haven — the home of a Manx
gay rights campaigner with a telephone that clicks.

When told to bend over backwards, he sighs
a sigh as they deem two noses enough, just now
they comb his pubic hair like a mine-filled beach
to declare it crab-free, and one could only wonder
if they really were looking for Mad Dog Magee.

Unabashed, the police park sheese y traid and accost
every single man visiting that home on Demesne Road.
Maybe they confessed to PC Roberts they'd shared chips,
cheese & gravy with Mad Dog Magee or dug a tunnel
behind the bread bin, with shakes of their left trouser leg.

sheese y traid : down the street

Death & Debts
after Camden's Britannia (1586)

an old manx custom	of claims settled
when a creditor laid	with his back
upon a grave	with his face
towards heaven	with his bible
bare-breasted	clutched too tightly
protesting so	lord's earth-bound
executors would repay	debts that stood
the unpaid sorrows	this ritual reclaims
unlike dark-glassed police	gods in lawful crimes
our demands clenched	to squeeze apologies
kneeling, not lying	facing self-filled tombs
gay men	that did not go to jail
who passed straight	to their grave
without prejudice	instead of freedom

Isle of Man Government

Hon. Howard Quayle MHK, Chief Minister
28 January 2020

███████████████████████████████████████
███████████████████████████████████████ it now seems incomprehensible that homosexuality was illegal on our Island until 1994. There was a time when consensual sexual activity between men in the privacy of their own homes was seen as a criminal activity warranting raids, searches and prosecution. ██████████████████ many of our countrymen were convicted as criminals simply for loving another adult. Many more lived in fear. Afraid to be honest about their identity to their friends, family and work colleagues. Forced to feel a sense of shame about who they were. ██████████████████████
We will never know the hurt our past laws ~~may~~ have inflicted on our own people. How many suffered. How many ~~perhaps~~ took their own lives. How many left their island never to return. The Bill before us today tries to right this historic wrong. It gives an automatic pardon to men convicted of homosexual activity.
██
████████████████████████████ Our previous laws discriminated against and criminalised men solely for who they were and who they loved. ███████████████ our previous laws were misguided and wrong. ██████████████ Those convicted should be seen as innocent. All those people affected the men themselves, their partners, wider family and friends. They deserve an unqualified apology from us. That apology can ~~only~~ come from the Government and from this House. ████████
██████████████████ ~~Our police and courts enforced the law at the time.~~ ████████████ Yet for decades this House tolerated and ignored this injustice. ████
I stand before you, before this House, before the people of our Island to apologise for those laws, for the damage they ~~may~~ have caused and lives they ruined. I am sorry for that wrong. Nothing I or we can do can erase past injustice.

Isle of Man Constabulary

Gary Roberts QPM, Chief Constable
22 July 2022

In many ways this is the most difficult letter that I have had to write

I have largely declined ~~to be pulled into a public debate about the need for me~~ to apologise for what the Isle of Man Constabulary did enforcing laws that outlawed homosexual acts between consenting adults.

Police officers ~~cannot~~ choose which laws to enforce they ~~cannot~~ have an opinion on the rightness or virtue of legislation, and they ~~must not~~ allow their personal opinions to affect how they work

~~injustice, prejudice and hatred.~~
large numbers of officers

I ~~also~~ worked with a ~~tiny~~ number, who were less tolerant and whose actions reflected values that were not in keeping with what the public ~~now~~ expects

the issue is not the narrow one about enforcement of the law but about how that was ~~sometimes~~ done…

It is a matter of deep and lasting regret to me that people feel the way the police treated them was so profoundly wrong as to make them fear, distrust or even hate the IOM Constabulary. ~~Whilst I cannot apologise for the act of enforcing the law~~ I can and will apologise for the way the law was ~~sometimes~~ enforced.

it is clear ~~that some of~~ the actions of the Constabulary caused distress to members of the gay community and their families. I regret that this was the case and I am sorry that ~~some~~ members of that community are still affected by this.

I admire the courage and determination shown by many people in the fight for gay rights. I have respect for Alan Shea and I can only begin to imagine how difficult things must have been for them That they have achieved so much should be a cause for celebration.

25

Joe Locke, Manx Actor

Isle of Pride
13 August 2022

I just want to send a little message to say how proud I am of our island, and how happy I am seeing the island celebrate its queer population. FINALLY!

It's time for all LGBTQ people to let their hair down and not care what some straight person thinks of your outfit. It's a day for all queer people to know they deserve the same love and respect that straight people get. for the people who don't feel comfortable in who they are, seeing a huge amount of people celebrating parts of themselves that society used to ridicule can change lives and bring out the confidence in people to become their true selves.

Pride started as a protest, from all around the world brave people standing up against oppression, brave people like our own Alan Shea He stood up for injustice when our own politicians within Tynwald were openly homophobic. Alan Shea, and so many LGBTQ people had to live in a society where the majority of their politicians didn't want to recognise their existence.

A quick read of Tynwald Hansard from the early 1990s exposes the rife homophobia in Tynwald with only Hazel Hannan and Allan Bell bravely fighting for LGBTQ rights in a room otherwise filled with bigots. One of the the things said by the bigots, Mrs Delaney, was right though.

She said, and I quote, "What they want, and they do not hide this, is for homosexuality to be treated just the same as heterosexuality. They want it to be taught in the schools, they want it to be recognised in the form of homosexual marriages. This is their aim."

Yes, Mrs Delaney, that was our aim, and that's what we got! Hmmm!

Young, Queer & Manx

Max, why's there so many men on your Instagram?
Max's mum

I have too many bad stories
there's a lot of bullying

school is hard
too much

the beach is the most free
at Scarlet we collect
lots of little weird things

like us

Puffins on the Calf
we forced them away
and now they want us back

Moddey Doo in Peel Castle

Here & Feared!
Fierce & Queer!

Squirrels — they look cute

everyone thinks
they are a pest

better to be a green sea turtle
the wren riding on the back of an eagle
a dragonfly

a chameleon because
sea horses are
peacocks are
everyone loves a ladybug

we have to be
really gay
the snazziest

caterpillars, the growth
it will come
a butterfly is just majestic
spreading its wings

Manx LGBT+ Legislative Timeline 1992–2022

1992 — Partial legalisation of sex between men passed, came into law in 1994.

— ~~Section 38 of the Sexual Offences Act 1992 made it illegal for "public bodies to promote homosexuality" thereby censoring LGBT existence.~~

2001 — Age of Consent for sex between men in private reduced to 18.

2006 — Age of Consent for sex between two men aligned to aged 16.

— Repeal of Section 38 of the Sexual Offences Act, 1992.

— LGBT Employment discrimination banned.

2009 — The right to change legal gender was introduced.

— Access to IVF for lesbian couples introduced.

2011 — Civil Partnerships for all couples were introduced.

— Joint adoption and stepchild adoption by same-sex couples.

2016 — Same-sex marriage legalised.

2017 — The Equality Act, which came into law in 2019, provided further protection from LGBT discrimination including goods and services.

2020 — IOM Government makes "unqualified apology" to gay men convicted of same-sex offences under previous Manx laws.

2021 — Historical gay sex offences were formally and automatically pardoned.

— Any therapy that attempts to change or suppress a person's sexual orientation or gender identity banned.

2022 — The Isle of Man Constabulary formally apologised for the way anti-gay laws were enforced and the impacts of that.

— IOM Government announced that blood donations by MSMs (men who have sex with men) would be allowed by law in early 2023.

— Hate Crime Bill plans to explicitly include "sexual orientation, civil partnership or marital status and gender reassignment".

Notes & Queeries

'Ware ye navar in love with a boy?'. For his Macmillan, UK collection F'o'c's'le Yarns (1881) TE Brown self-censored various "coarse" passages including this one from the original Betsy Lee (1872). The poem uses both words from the original text and the author's own.

i.m. Dursley James McLinden
Dursley James McLinden (b. 29 May 1965. d. 7 August 1995) was a Manx actor, dancer, singer and magician, who died in London of AIDS-related illness. He was an inspiration for the character Ritchie Tozer, played by Olly Alexander, in the Channel 4 drama *It's A Sin*.

'Bells & Bells' and **'Poem in August at 5pm'** were partly inspired by stories in *Love from the Pink Palace* by Jill Nalder (Wildfire, 2022). Dursley McLinden died at 5pm on 7 August. Dursley asked his friend Niko to give a reading at the funeral and he chose Lorca's poem 'A las cinco de la tarde'.

'i could have been you' makes *italicised* references to shows Dursley acted in. The author was also born in Noble's Hospital, Douglas (10 December 1965).

'Remembrance of the Daleks & Other Supernatural Creatures'. Dursley played Sergeant Mike Smith in the *Doctor Who* serial 'Remembrance of the Daleks' (5–26 October 1988) with Sylvester McCoy as the Doctor.

'Life was a Trapdoor'. Refers to six types of trapdoor devices in theatres. The Gaiety Theatre and Opera House, Douglas has one of the last working Corsican trapdoors, along with a rare Liquid Dimmer for lighting.

'A politician walks into a mirrored room'. The Department of Health says it doesn't know how many HIV cases there are on the Isle of Man and has no plans to publish HIV statistics, claiming it could lead to patients being identified (*Manx Radio*, 12 June 2013). It is claimed that "certain senior Manx politicians" are not acknowledging the true HIV position because "it would show the island in a bad light" according to Tony, IOM HIV Support Group (*Manx Radio*, 12 July 2013). Manx Care says it doesn't know how many people test positive for HIV on the IOM after a freedom of information request (*3FM*, 14 March 2022).

Isle of Man Queer History (1986–92). Alan Shea (b. 1963) is the IOM's leading gay rights campaigner. He was a member of the Ellan Vannin Gay Group in the 1980s and 90s along with his long-term partner, later husband, Stephen Moore. They were primarily responsible for the partial legalisation of sex between men in 1992. Alan has continued to campaign ever since, especially for the police apology achieved in 2022.

'MOAS (Manx Opposed to Alan Shea) Manifesto, 1991', 'Standing in his yard looking like Liberace in a velvet jacket'. Mel Cheetham (d. 4 May 2020) was believed to be a founder of MOAS. He was featured and pictured in an article 'Mad Manx' (*The Independent Magazine*, 1 June 1991) in his stoneyard. He actively sought male support for MOAS, "*I stop at roadsides where I see fellows digging the road. The rougher the fellows are the more keen they are*".

'Bona Vacantia'. Frank and Dorothy Duggan were "*furious proselytising*" homophobes. Frank claimed, "*Legalise them and there will be no limit. Soon they'll want marriage and then to adopt children and the age of consent will get lower: 18, 16, 14, 12 — until it becomes paedophilia*". ('Mad Manx' *ibid.*) The Duggans were satirised in *The Fast Show* (BBC in 1994-97, 2000 and 2014). Caravans were then only allowed on the island with a special licence.

'Pride & Protest'. "I would birch homosexuals" is a quote by Mel Cheetham. "Bum blasters, dirty filthy buggery" was said by an unidentified Manxman at the Opening of Tynwald, 5 July 1991 when Alan Shea handed in a Petition for Redress to legalise male homosexual sexual acts. It was organised by the Ellan Vannin Gay Group, supported by Peter Tatchell's Outrage! which appeared in a documentary, *The Rites of Man* with Sir Ian McKellen.

"Wimps & perverts infect society further" is a quote from Mr RE Quine, MHK in 1987. Allan Bell also said in this debate, "There be few more awesome sights in life than bigotry, ignorance and hypocrisy united in moral outrage". Allan was a key supporter of the decriminalisation of sex between men from 1987 as was fellow Member of the House of Keys, Hazel Hannan (MHK 1986-2006). As Chief Minister, Allan led the equalisation of the age of consent, gay adoption, gay civil partnerships and gay marriage.

Successive Bishops of Sodor and Man, ex officio members of the Legislative Council, voted against the partial legalisation of sex between men, including when it was passed in 1992.

'Pink & Blue', 'Death & Debts', 'The Knock', 'Believe it — or not', 'Any Excuse'. Robin Oake, Chief Constable of IOM Constabulary 1986-1999, was formerly the Assistant Chief Constable to James Anderton in the UK — infamous for zealous police tactics in dealing with queer men fuelled by his religious beliefs and stated view in 1987 that "male sodomy should be illegal".

After Oake's appointment gay & bi men in the Isle of Man were subjected to surveillance and harassment including secret CCTV cameras and entrapment in public toilets. Oake, a member of the Order of St John, said he did not believe the Manx law should be changed. Police were accused of abuse, harassment, blackmail, the denial of legal support and illegal confinement. The treatment of gay & bi men, during this period, including whilst in police custody, was investigated by Amnesty International in 1992.

'**Death & Debts**' was inspired by an old Manx custom in Camden's Britannia (1586 edition) by William Camden (1551-1623).

In '**Believe it — or not**' the reference The Beverley Sisters was the local nickname for the "pretty boy policemen" used as entrapment bait in Earl's Court, as mentioned by Rupert Everett in the Channel 4 documentary *Fifty Shades of Gay*.

'**Any Excuse**' is inspired by a police raid and surveillance of Alan Shea's home.

'**Isle of Man Government — Howard Quayle MHK**'. Extracts and erasures from a speech by The Chief Minister apologising for the laws and the impacts of the laws criminalising sex between men. He announced a Bill granting automatic pardons for male homosexual offences, albeit the police later announced they had lost the records of such offences.

'**Isle of Man Constabulary — Gary Roberts QPM**'. Extracts and erasures from the Chief Constable's letter of 22 July 2022 apologising for the way that laws were enforced against gay men. This apology is unprecedented, despite similar policies and tactics being used in the UK, especially throughout the 1950s to 1970s.

'**Joe Locke, Manx Actor — Heartstopper**'. In this speech, Joe also appealed to the Manx government to pass legislation allowing 'men who have sex with men' to donate blood. The following day a promise was given to pass this legislation in early 2023.

'**Young, Queer & Manx**'. Found poem with thanks to Douglas LGBTQ Youth Group, Ramsey LGBTQ Youth Group and to Bean, Elijah, Ely, Grey, Kerrie, Leanne, Max Vernon (and Max's mum), Shawn, Sheena and Zen for sharing their experiences of living queer on the island.

The Calf is the Calf of Man, a nature sanctuary island off the south coast of the Isle of Man, where puffins were driven away by rodents, but are now being lured back.

Moddey Doo [Manx Gaelic: Black Dog] is a phantom black hound in Manx folklore that haunted Peel Castle leaving all the soldiers in great fear.

Acknowledgements

Previous versions of 'Pride & Protest', 'Pink & Blue', 'Death & Debts' appear in the chapbook *Throatbone* (UnCollected Press, 2020) and *The Raw Art Review*, Summer Issue, 2020.

'Any Excuse' appeared in *Ink Sweat & Tears*, 27 October 2022.

'a politician walks into a mirrored room' appears in *Impossible Archetype Journal*, Issue 13, April 2023.

'Standing in his yard looking like Liberace in a velvet jacket' appeared in *Island Life*, *Manx Independent*, 23 February 2023.

Thank You

Immense gratitude to Peter Collins at Polari Press for supporting this publication to help give light to these queer histories. Thanks to all those who provided supportive quotes for the book and social media.

Thanks also to those who supported the creation of these poems: Brighton Poetry Stanza, Covent Garden Poetry Stanza, The Crocodile Collective, Culture Vannin, Douglas LGBTQ Youth Group, Gef the Mongoose, Rob Hamberger, Mari Hughes-Edwards, Ruth Keggin Gell, Martin Lyons, Breesha Maddrell, Manx Museum, Manx LitFest, Stephen Moore, New Writing South, Caleb Parkin, Ramsey LGBTQ Youth Group, Royal Literary Fund, Alan Shea, Chris Sheard, SKEGS, Society of Authors.

The price of queer freedom is eternal vigilance
— Peter Tatchell